STECK-VAUGHN

Comprehension

CONTEXT

LEVEL
C

Linda Ward Beech
Tara McCarthy
Donna Townsend

SOUTH SHORE MIDDLE SCHOOL

STECK-VAUGHN
C O M P A N Y
A Subsidiary of National Education Corporation

Executive Editor:	Diane Sharpe
Project Editor:	Melinda Veatch
Senior Editor:	Anne Rose Souby
Design Coordinator:	Sharon Golden
Project Design:	Howard Adkins Communications
Cover Illustration:	Rhonda Childress
Photographs:	©Jane Grushow /Grant Heilman (plant)
	©Photo Reseachers

ISBN 0-8114-7839-4

4 5 6 7 8 9 0 VP 96

Using context is a way to learn new words. You can learn a new word by looking at the words around it. In this book you will learn how to use context.

What is context? Suppose you want a tomato. If you live in the country, you might go to a garden. If you live in the city, you might go to a store. In the context of the country, tomatoes are in gardens. In the context of the city, tomatoes are in stores.

What Is Context?

Context means all the words in a sentence or all the sentences in a paragraph. If you find a word you do not know, look at the words around it. These other words can help you figure out what the word means.

Try It!

Read the paragraph below. It has a word that you may not know. The word is printed in **dark letters**. See whether you can find out what the word means.

◆

Sheena's best friend gave her a present. It looked like a book on the outside. But the pages were blank. It was a **diary**. Sheena liked the idea of making her own book. She writes in it every day. She writes about her family and friends. She writes about training her dog.

If you don't know what **diary** means, look at the context. This paragraph contains these words:

Clue: looked like a book on the outside

Clue: the pages were blank

Clue: Sheena liked the idea of making her own book.

Find these clues in the paragraph. Draw a circle around them. What words do you think of when you read the clues? Write the words below:

Did you write *journal*? The context clue words tell you that a **diary** is a journal or record of what you do every day.

Using What You Know

Below are some paragraphs with words left out. Read the paragraphs. Look at the context. Then fill in the blanks with words about you.

I once had a pet named _____ . It was a

_____ . We got it when I was _____

years old. I used to love to _____ with my

_____ .

My favorite kind of music is _____ . I especially

like _____ . If I could, I would learn to play the

_____ .

I like to spend time _____ . My favorite

_____ is _____ . If I could, I would

_____ .

I like to go to the _____ . When I get there,

I always _____ and _____ . My

_____ also likes to go to the _____ .

I like to watch _____ on TV. It is

_____ and _____ . My favorite

character is _____ .

Working with Context

This book asks questions that you can answer by using context clues in paragraphs. There are two kinds of paragraphs. The paragraphs in the first part of this book have blank spaces in them. You can use the context clues in the paragraphs to decide which word should go in each space. Here is an example:

◆

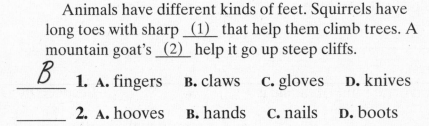

Animals have different kinds of feet. Squirrels have long toes with sharp __(1)__ that help them climb trees. A mountain goat's __(2)__ help it go up steep cliffs.

_____ **1.** **A.** fingers   **B.** claws   **C.** gloves   **D.** knives

_____ **2.** **A.** hooves   **B.** hands   **C.** nails   **D.** boots

Look at the answer choices for blank 1. Treat the paragraph as a puzzle. Which pieces don't fit? Which piece fits best? Try putting each word in the blank. See which one makes the most sense. Squirrels don't have sharp *fingers* or *gloves* or *knives*. *Claws* (answer **B**) is the only choice that makes sense. Now try to answer question 2 on your own.

The paragraphs in the second part of this book are different. For these you figure out the meaning of a word that is printed in **dark letters** in the paragraph. Here is an example:

◆

Eskimos use **kayaks** to travel the icy waters where they live. Kayaks are like canoes, but they have room for only one person.

The word in dark type is **kayaks**. Find the context clues. Then choose a word that means the same as **kayaks**.

_____ **3.** In this paragraph, the word **kayaks** means

    A. sleds   **C.** boats

    B. skis   **D.** planes

To check your answers, turn to page 62.

How to Use This Book

Read the stories in this book. If a word in a story is missing, choose the word that fits. If there is a word in dark letters in a story, figure out what that word means.

You can check your answers by looking at pages 59 through 61. Write the number of correct answers in the score box at the top of the page. After you finish all the stories, turn to pages 56 through 58. Work through "Think and Apply." The answers to those questions are on page 62.

Hints for Better Reading

- Keep reading, even if you come to a word you do not know.
- When you finish reading, look at each answer choice. The right answer is the word that goes with the other words in the story.
- If you can't find the answer the first time, look back at the story. Then try the answer choices again.

Challenge Yourself

Try this. Make a list of all the words printed in dark letters. Write a sentence using each one.

Unit 1

The condor is dying out. Only 27 of these large birds are still living. A few years ago, some people raised condors in a zoo. They took two eggs from condor nests. The eggs __(1)__ . Now the baby birds live in the zoo. It will take __(2)__ years for the birds to grow up. Then they will be turned loose.

_____ **1.** **A.** sang **B.** behaved **C.** locked **D.** hatched

_____ **2.** **A.** several **B.** bad **C.** bent **D.** deep

Some wasps build their nests out of paper. They chew wood. They __(3)__ it with juice in their mouths. Then they __(4)__ out the wet mixture and make their nests.

_____ **3.** **A.** mix **B.** paste **C.** hurt **D.** bake

_____ **4.** **A.** kick **B.** spit **C.** shoot **D.** hug

Magic Johnson is a basketball superstar. He practiced every day when he was a __(5)__ . He practiced bouncing the ball. He practiced __(6)__ the ball. Magic says that it's hard to practice every day. But that's how to become a winner!

_____ **5.** **A.** teacher **B.** coach **C.** batter **D.** youth

_____ **6.** **A.** sliding **B.** hunting **C.** shooting **D.** sitting

A guide dog is helpful to a blind person. The dog wears a __(7)__ with a long handle. The blind person holds the handle. Then the person gives __(8)__ . The dog obeys them. It carefully guides the blind person across streets.

_____ **7.** **A.** coat **B.** harness **C.** shirt **D.** belt

_____ **8.** **A.** fences **B.** jars **C.** toys **D.** commands

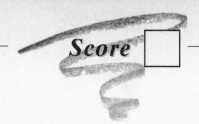
People once recorded events on a stick. Each town had a stick keeper. This person would cut pictures into the stick. The pictures showed __(9)__ things that happened during the year. The stick helped people remember the __(10)__ .

_____ **9. A.** important   **B.** crazy   **C.** easy   **D.** narrow

_____ **10. A.** path   **B.** roof   **C.** past   **D.** song

Mother's Day has been celebrated for a very long time. But the first Father's Day wasn't celebrated until 1910. Sonora Dodd got her city to __(11)__ fathers on June 19. Then 62 years later, Father's Day became a __(12)__ holiday.

_____ **11. A.** feed   **B.** honor   **C.** picture   **D.** moan

_____ **12. A.** national   **B.** sunny   **C.** busy   **D.** straight

Joe Louis was one of the __(13)__ boxers. He was the best in the country for 12 years. Most boxers are not strong enough to fight so long. Joe finally stopped fighting in 1949. The next year he tried to make a __(14)__ . But he lost the fight.

_____ **13. A.** careful   **B.** weakest   **C.** greatest   **D.** summer

_____ **14. A.** bench   **B.** mess   **C.** sled   **D.** comeback

The chipmunk __(15)__ from place to place looking for food. It gathers nuts, fruit, and berries all summer. The chipmunk stores its food for the winter. It hides the food in the underground __(16)__ where it lives.

_____ **15. A.** sleeps   **B.** pays   **C.** darts   **D.** trembles

_____ **16. A.** tunnels   **B.** roots   **C.** inns   **D.** years

Unit 2

People in Russia give eggs as gifts. They do not give just plain white eggs. The eggs are painted with pictures. Many of the pictures have __(1)__ meanings, such as "good luck" and "long life." In Russia __(2)__ eggs become little works of art!

_____ **1.** **A.** special   **B.** cold   **C.** small   **D.** purple

_____ **2.** **A.** lizard   **B.** ordinary   **C.** red   **D.** broken

---

A man wondered whether bees know which flowers to go to. So he drew flowers on a large __(3)__ of paper. Half the flowers were blue. The other half were yellow. On each blue flower, he put a big cup of sugar water. But he put a __(4)__ cup on each yellow flower. The bees stopped going to the yellow flowers.

_____ **3.** **A.** test   **B.** row   **C.** sheet   **D.** pencil

_____ **4.** **A.** big   **B.** tiny   **C.** glass   **D.** slow

---

Some plants don't have seeds. So how can you grow a seedless grape plant? First cut off a piece of __(5)__ from a grape plant. Put it in water. Soon it begins to grow roots. Plant it in the __(6)__ . It will grow into a new grape plant.

_____ **5.** **A.** stem   **B.** tree   **C.** spoon   **D.** stone

_____ **6.** **A.** step   **B.** dirt   **C.** green   **D.** road

---

Sounds can move through air or water. Sounds bounce back if they hit a __(7)__ object. Then you can hear them a second time. These __(8)__ sounds are called echoes.

_____ **7.** **A.** solid   **B.** mean   **C.** burned   **D.** eager

_____ **8.** **A.** fair   **B.** forty   **C.** pink   **D.** repeated

Animals have different ways to escape from (9) . Some run very fast. Others climb trees. But some are safe because they are hard to see. They may be the same color as the ground. Or they may look like plants. They may have (10) or spots that look like the shadows of trees. Instead of running, these animals stand very still.

_____ **9. A.** mice   **B.** danger   **C.** clouds   **D.** help

_____ **10. A.** stripes   **B.** teeth   **C.** string   **D.** soup

---

Every year in Thailand, people have Elephant Day. They bring their elephants to one (11) . Everyone comes to see whose elephant is the best. The elephants run a race. They also carry big logs and (12) them in a pile.

_____ **11. A.** bit   **B.** fault   **C.** location   **D.** paper

_____ **12. A.** think   **B.** climb   **C.** stack   **D.** sneeze

---

Have you ever (13) a pill bug? These animals are not pills or bugs! They got the name *pill* because they can roll up into a ball. They got the name *bug* because of their small (14) . But they belong to the same family as crabs.

_____ **13. A.** counted   **B.** run   **C.** cried   **D.** observed

_____ **14. A.** answers   **B.** size   **C.** day   **D.** park

---

A giant toad finds (15) in a cool, damp place. At night the toad comes out. It needs food for its huge (16) . The toad eats as many insects as it can find.

_____ **15. A.** cows   **B.** magic   **C.** money   **D.** shelter

_____ **16. A.** leg   **B.** appetite   **C.** suit   **D.** rule

Unit 3

A hummingbird eats 180 times a day. Every meal is a big one. The tiny bird eats one fortieth of its body __(1)__ at each meal. That is like a human being drinking a __(2)__ of orange juice for a snack.

_____ 1. **A.** feast   **B.** house   **C.** weight   **D.** wheat

_____ 2. **A.** gallon   **B.** plate   **C.** piece   **D.** sandwich

---

Batman is a comic-book hero. There is a real batman, though. He __(3)__ bats in his home. He says the animals are smart and __(4)__ . He also says they can be trained just like dogs.

_____ 3. **A.** writes   **B.** raises   **C.** plays   **D.** swallows

_____ 4. **A.** fresh   **B.** salty   **C.** rainy   **D.** gentle

---

People have used __(5)__ to guess the weather for many years. But experts and these machines are right only some of the time. Perhaps the best way to guess the weather is to __(6)__ the sky.

_____ 5. **A.** gas   **B.** sticks   **C.** computers   **D.** groups

_____ 6. **A.** study   **B.** paint   **C.** drive   **D.** clap

---

Long ago, people often __(7)__ to hot springs. There, warm water __(8)__ from the earth. People thought the special water would make them healthy.

_____ 7. **A.** lived   **B.** traveled   **C.** belonged   **D.** worked

_____ 8. **A.** called   **B.** bubbled   **C.** grew   **D.** fished

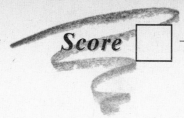
People who like to __(9)__ caves are called spelunkers. To become a spelunker, it is best to begin going with __(10)__. They take people safely through caves.

_____ 9. **A.** take **B.** spin **C.** explore **D.** decide

_____ 10. **A.** noises **B.** surprises **C.** storms **D.** guides

---

The people of South America built beautiful homes 1,900 years ago. Their homes were made of stone. The kitchen was in a __(11)__ building. In the sleeping __(12)__, the beds were built into a wall.

_____ 11. **A.** mad **B.** separate **C.** polite **D.** fast

_____ 12. **A.** fish **B.** prairie **C.** chamber **D.** farm

---

Jim Sundberg's bat went whack! The ball flew high above the fielder's glove. It was a home run. Later, people measured the baseball __(13)__. Someone had drawn the lines wrong. If the lines had been drawn __(14)__, the hit would have been a foul ball, and the other team may have won.

_____ 13. **A.** cat **B.** glove **C.** diamond **D.** bottom

_____ 14. **A.** alone **B.** correctly **C.** wrong **D.** ugly

---

Saturn was named for the Roman god of farming. This great __(15)__ is famous for the rings around it. The seven main rings are made up of huge __(16)__ of ice.

_____ 15. **A.** planet **B.** mud **C.** club **D.** pond

_____ 16. **A.** maps **B.** drinks **C.** chunks **D.** tubs

Our __(1)__ for sending letters has changed over the years. A long time ago, people just folded their letters and used wax to close them. Also, the person who sent the letter did not pay for it. Instead, the __(2)__ had to pay.

_____ 1. **A.** mailbox   **B.** address   **C.** system   **D.** van

_____ 2. **A.** sender   **B.** receiver   **C.** sister   **D.** sailor

Many plants grow from seed. Plants have different ways of __(3)__ their seeds. A bluebonnet has seeds in a __(4)__ . When the plant dries, it can shoot its seeds fifty feet!

_____ 3. **A.** trying   **B.** baking   **C.** shopping   **D.** sowing

_____ 4. **A.** purse   **B.** boat   **C.** pod   **D.** bag

A man __(5)__ a piece of art that looked real. He wrapped a woman in cloth. Next he put a kind of paste on the cloth. When the paste dried, the cloth was very hard. Then the man cut the cloth open. The woman got out. The man had a __(6)__ of the woman's shape. Then he put clay inside the shape. When the clay got hard, he took it out and painted it. The clay woman looked real!

_____ 5. **A.** walked   **B.** formed   **C.** wrote   **D.** sank

_____ 6. **A.** mold   **B.** dress   **C.** drawing   **D.** painting

Moss is a __(7)__ green plant. It is soft. It grows on trees, rocks, and soil. The earth __(8)__ from moss in many ways. Moss breaks rocks down into soil. Moss holds water in the ground.

_____ 7. **A.** full   **B.** fun   **C.** tender   **D.** new

_____ 8. **A.** pours   **B.** throws   **C.** sees   **D.** benefits

A man used an airplane to cover his gas __(9)__. He hoped people would then stop to buy gas. He bought a B-17 airplane. It took three big machines to __(10)__ the plane onto poles. Then he put lights under the wings. People could look up at the plane while they filled up.

_____ **9.** **A.** well   **B.** hole   **C.** tank   **D.** station

_____ **10.** **A.** fly   **B.** elevate   **C.** begin   **D.** drive

---

Turtles __(11)__ to be very slow animals. But many turtles are really very __(12)__. Sea turtles can swim quickly. The green turtle can swim as fast as twenty miles per hour for a short time.

_____ **11.** **A.** appear   **B.** alarm   **C.** nibble   **D.** hide

_____ **12.** **A.** young   **B.** huge   **C.** plain   **D.** speedy

---

Some people think Lincoln wrote the Gettysburg Address on a __(13)__ of paper. This is __(14)__. He wrote it carefully on a whole sheet of paper. He changed the words four times. Every time he changed the words, he copied it over again.

_____ **13.** **A.** letter   **B.** scrap   **C.** ship   **D.** chain

_____ **14.** **A.** incorrect   **B.** sad   **C.** large   **D.** useful

---

The moray eel lives in warm ocean waters. It is a strong fish with very sharp teeth. The eel hides in a hole or cave. It can catch fish with __(15)__ speed. The moray eel will not __(16)__ out from its hole to look for food until it is night.

_____ **15.** **A.** brave   **B.** dry   **C.** lightning   **D.** half

_____ **16.** **A.** blink   **B.** venture   **C.** list   **D.** roll

Gentle Jungle is a __(1)__ school for animals. There they learn how to act for movies and TV. The __(2)__ teach lions, bears, and monkeys. They even teach snakes and spiders!

_____ **1. A.** cleaning **B.** walking **C.** thinking **D.** training

_____ **2. A.** children **B.** actors **C.** instructors **D.** twins

---

People who go to the Rock of Gibraltar may see a band of monkeys. The monkeys have been there for many years. People believe they are good luck. __(3)__ , the monkeys can also be a lot of trouble. They are very __(4)__ . They can open bags. They can even press the buttons on cameras.

_____ **3. A.** Whenever **B.** So **C.** Since **D.** However

_____ **4. A.** smart **B.** worried **C.** shy **D.** scary

A man made a new kind of flying toy. It looks like a ring. It works like an airplane wing. The top is bent. It is flat __(5)__ . The __(6)__ sticks up a bit. This makes the toy fly straight. The man wanted this toy to fly farther than other toys. It has been thrown as far as three football fields!

_____ **5. A.** above **B.** forever **C.** often **D.** underneath

_____ **6. A.** rim **B.** handle **C.** head **D.** mouth

Pearl Bailey said that it's never too late. She won singing prizes. She had many fans. She acted in movies. She wrote books. But she never __(7)__ college. At the age of sixty, she began. She chose an __(8)__ school and started taking classes!

_____ **7. A.** learned **B.** attended **C.** picked **D.** ran

_____ **8. A.** awful **B.** angry **C.** excellent **D.** ill

Have you ever heard of the game *polocrosse*? It comes from polo and lacrosse. As in polo, players ride horses. As in lacrosse, players use long sticks with small nets to catch a ball. The player with the ball __(9)__ down a long field. The player can score by __(10)__ the ball between two poles.

_____ **9.** **A.** hops   **B.** kicks   **C.** charges   **D.** skips

_____ **10.** **A.** hurling   **B.** seeing   **C.** choosing   **D.** guessing

An oyster is an animal that lives in the sea. When it's born, it looks like a tiny lump. It floats and swims for two weeks. Next its shell __(11)__ . Then the oyster __(12)__ on an object. The oyster fastens itself to the object. It doesn't move again.

_____ **11.** **A.** wins   **B.** hardens   **C.** whispers   **D.** shines

_____ **12.** **A.** lifts   **B.** naps   **C.** settles   **D.** shops

Living stones are desert plants. They are __(13)__ to Africa. Some living stones grow under the sand. Only parts of their leaves are __(14)__ to the sun. Others look like small rocks until they flower.

_____ **13.** **A.** kind   **B.** native   **C.** little   **D.** second

_____ **14.** **A.** over   **B.** made   **C.** exposed   **D.** next

The North Star is called Polaris. It __(15)__ in the night sky above the North Pole. This makes it easy to find in the sky. Also, this star is easy to find since it is so __(16)__ . Many people have used it to tell which way is north.

_____ **15.** **A.** eats   **B.** drops   **C.** twinkles   **D.** blackens

_____ **16.** **A.** old   **B.** dazzling   **C.** far   **D.** stupid

Chicks talk to their mothers even before they leave the egg. The chicks peep while inside their eggshells. The hens hear the noise. They __(1)__ their babies. __(2)__ the chicks crack their eggs open. It's hard work, so they get very tired. But their mothers' voices help them come into the world at last.

_____ 1. **A.** leave   **B.** wish   **C.** answer   **D.** become

_____ 2. **A.** Since   **B.** Gradually   **C.** Proudly   **D.** Nearly

---

Thailand is a country with many rivers. Some villages even have rivers instead of streets. People shop at floating __(3)__ . Many of the stores are boats. The boats look like __(4)__ . But they are wider and flatter on the bottom.

_____ 3. **A.** stories   **B.** houses   **C.** markets   **D.** classes

_____ 4. **A.** canoes   **B.** birds   **C.** kites   **D.** dogs

---

John Cage writes songs that sound very strange to most people. His songs are played with whistles, radios, cans, and shells. The strangest song John Cage has written is "Four Minutes and Thirty-Three __(5)__ ." In this song a __(6)__ just sits for that long without ever playing a note!

_____ 5. **A.** People   **B.** Times   **C.** Seconds   **D.** Clocks

_____ 6. **A.** writer   **B.** fan   **C.** loaf   **D.** musician

---

If you look in the night sky, you may see the Milky Way. It looks like a __(7)__ , white band. There are __(8)__ of bright stars in the Milky Way.

_____ 7. **A.** smart   **B.** hazy   **C.** bushy   **D.** safe

_____ 8. **A.** trays   **B.** roads   **C.** billions   **D.** racks

Totem poles are tall wooden poles with animals painted on them. The animals look __(9)__ . Parts of them look like people. One part of each animal sticks out. Bears have huge claws. Beavers have long front teeth. Crows have long, straight __(10)__ .

_____ **9.** **A.** better   **B.** unreal   **C.** orange   **D.** unhappy

_____ **10.** **A.** noses   **B.** arms   **C.** buttons   **D.** beaks

---

The first Ferris wheel was taller than a twenty-story building. George Ferris made the giant wheel ride for the 1893 World's Fair. It had 36 cars. It held many __(11)__ . At the top of the wheel, everyone could see for __(12)__ .

_____ **11.** **A.** passengers   **B.** puppets   **C.** rulers   **D.** balls

_____ **12.** **A.** glasses   **B.** animals   **C.** miles   **D.** hours

---

The numbat has sharp claws on its front feet. The numbat uses these to tear open __(13)__ logs. Then it puts its long, sticky __(14)__ inside to catch termites. A numbat eats only termites.

_____ **13.** **A.** yellow   **B.** square   **C.** red   **D.** rotten

_____ **14.** **A.** brain   **B.** tongue   **C.** fin   **D.** eye

---

There is gold in ocean water. The __(15)__ is getting it out. Since the gold there is __(16)__ , taking it out of the ocean costs a lot of money. Maybe one day someone will find an easy way to do it.

_____ **15.** **A.** bank   **B.** team   **C.** number   **D.** problem

_____ **16.** **A.** scarce   **B.** light   **C.** free   **D.** nickel

Abebe Bikila ran in a 26-mile race. He __(1)__ new shoes for the race. They hurt his feet. So he took them off and kept running. Near the end his __(2)__ feet really hurt. Yet he was the first ever to finish the race in only two hours!

_____ **1. A.** broke **B.** painted **C.** wore **D.** tripped

_____ **2. A.** wild **B.** bare **C.** silent **D.** clown

The moose looks funny. It has a big nose and a lot of skin flapping under its chin. It has four toes on each __(3)__ . It has big __(4)__ , long legs, and almost no tail. But it is the biggest and strongest kind of deer.

_____ **3. A.** hand **B.** arm **C.** hoof **D.** horn

_____ **4. A.** shoulders **B.** wings **C.** fingers **D.** words

Sand paintings are made with colored sand. They show animals or people. Native Americans make them on the ground at __(5)__ times of the year. But these sand paintings don't last long. The wind __(6)__ them away.

_____ **5. A.** minutes **B.** certain **C.** still **D.** worse

_____ **6. A.** whisks **B.** pulls **C.** breaks **D.** drives

Sunlight has many colors. It's __(7)__ to see them because they are mixed to make white light. But when white light enters a drop of water, something happens. The light bounces off the inside of a drop. It is bent __(8)__ you. The white light splits apart into colors. Then you see a rainbow.

_____ **7. A.** different **B.** impossible **C.** able **D.** fast

_____ **8. A.** after **B.** toward **C.** through **D.** from

Harriet Tubman was a slave who escaped to __(9)__ in the North. She worried about the slaves still in the South, so she returned many times. Each time, she helped slaves escape. A huge __(10)__ was offered to anyone who caught her. But no one ever did.

_____ **9.** **A.** nowhere   **B.** rains   **C.** us   **D.** freedom

_____ **10.** **A.** reward   **B.** trunk   **C.** cave   **D.** seal

---

In the spring some fish leave the __(11)__ where they live. They swim __(12)__ in rivers to ponds where they were born. These fish can find their way even when their eyes are covered. But they get lost if their noses are covered. The fish use their noses to find their way!

_____ **11.** **A.** ocean   **B.** valley   **C.** basket   **D.** leaf

_____ **12.** **A.** everywhere   **B.** hardly   **C.** upstream   **D.** here

---

Puffins are birds that live on northern coasts. __(13)__ of puffins stay at sea most of the time. They swim and dive to catch fish. They come on land to nest on high __(14)__ .

_____ **13.** **A.** Pans   **B.** Friends   **C.** Flocks   **D.** Barns

_____ **14.** **A.** cliffs   **B.** seas   **C.** nets   **D.** pits

---

Smog is usually a mix of smoke and fog. It can also come from the sun acting on __(15)__ in the air. Smog can __(16)__ a person's health and kill plant life. Smog can be very thick, making it hard to see things.

_____ **15.** **A.** stars   **B.** fumes   **C.** pals   **D.** pens

_____ **16.** **A.** fix   **B.** save   **C.** give   **D.** damage

The Mummer's Parade is on New Year's Day in Philadelphia. Thousands of people __(1)__ in the parade. They dress in __(2)__ clothes. Bands play merry songs. People dance down the street. The parade lasts all day long.

_____ **1.** **A.** visit   **B.** march   **C.** guess   **D.** faint

_____ **2.** **A.** wild   **B.** hard   **C.** curly   **D.** wet

The first string of Christmas tree lights was made about one hundred years ago. It was made by hand. The lights all __(3)__ on and off. Soon the idea caught on. Many people wanted the lights. So some __(4)__ started to make them.

_____ **3.** **A.** heard   **B.** hopped   **C.** winked   **D.** felt

_____ **4.** **A.** lights   **B.** spiders   **C.** companies   **D.** plugs

The queen of England has a doll house. But it is more like a doll __(5)__ ! It has running water. The lights can be turned off and on. The elevator works. The piano plays __(6)__ . The doll house would be great for a queen who was five inches tall!

_____ **5.** **A.** face   **B.** castle   **C.** shoe   **D.** baby

_____ **6.** **A.** ball   **B.** games   **C.** pool   **D.** music

Pablo Picasso was a busy __(7)__ . First he learned about art from his father. Then he began painting when he was 9 years old. When Pablo was 13, he started to study at an important art school. In his life he did thousands of __(8)__ and paintings. He was still working when he died at age 93.

_____ **7.** **A.** girl   **B.** driver   **C.** singer   **D.** artist

_____ **8.** **A.** places   **B.** drawings   **C.** chairs   **D.** ideas

Peanut butter was first made by George Washington Carver. He __(9)__ many other ways to use peanuts, too. Carver wanted to help farmers. He hoped they could make money raising peanuts. His wish came true. Farmers started making money. And kids started __(10)__ peanut butter!

_____ **9.** **A.** carried   **B.** discovered   **C.** filled   **D.** raked

_____ **10.** **A.** enjoying   **B.** losing   **C.** wearing   **D.** drinking

---

In Florida it's too warm for snow. So one year people there had a Snow Day. They got a snow machine. The machine made a snow pile that was two __(11)__ high. The people had so much fun they __(12)__ to have a Snow Day every year.

_____ **11.** **A.** plants   **B.** heads   **C.** books   **D.** stories

_____ **12.** **A.** decided   **B.** believed   **C.** blinked   **D.** drove

---

Dark __(13)__ on the sun are called sunspots. They look dark because they are cooler than the rest of the sun. Large spots may take weeks to fade away, while small ones __(14)__ in just hours.

_____ **13.** **A.** patches   **B.** dust   **C.** kits   **D.** leaves

_____ **14.** **A.** remember   **B.** swim   **C.** vanish   **D.** use

---

Water lilies grow year after year. Their roots __(15)__ to the bottom of a lake or stream. Their large leaves float. Strong stems hold the flowers above water. Some water lilies bloom during the day. Others bloom __(16)__ at night.

_____ **15.** **A.** see   **B.** cling   **C.** thaw   **D.** pierce

_____ **16.** **A.** loudly   **B.** solely   **C.** wisely   **D.** barely

It pays to go to __(1)__ . People who go can make better __(2)__ than those who don't. Someone who finishes high school may make five dollars for one hour's work. A person who finishes college may make much more for that same hour!

_____ **1. A.** camp   **B.** college   **C.** church   **D.** jail

_____ **2. A.** sons   **B.** aunts   **C.** wages   **D.** rakers

---

In some cold places, people like dog-sled racing. Special dogs pull the sleds. The dogs must be strong so they can run for a long time without __(3)__ . They must be smart enough to follow the orders __(4)__ to them during a race.

_____ **3. A.** winning   **B.** tiring   **C.** hitting   **D.** breathing

_____ **4. A.** shouted   **B.** passed   **C.** taken   **D.** thrown

---

Long ago, Highway 1 was used by people riding __(5)__ . It was __(6)__ as the Boston Post Road then. People used it to go from Boston to New York. It took them two weeks to get there. Today the drive would take about five hours.

_____ **5. A.** ahead   **B.** funny   **C.** behind   **D.** horseback

_____ **6. A.** ended   **B.** known   **C.** given   **D.** sold

---

Small streams run over rocks. Sometimes streams run through a crack in the rocks. Then the stream runs down __(7)__ . Over thousands of years, the water wears the rocks away. A __(8)__ place is made. After a long time, it is big enough to stand in. That is how a cave is made.

_____ **7. A.** away   **B.** together   **C.** apart   **D.** underground

_____ **8. A.** cool   **B.** high   **C.** hollow   **D.** true

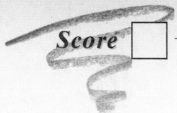
A magnet can be a piece of stone or metal. Magnets come in a __(9)__ of shapes and sizes. They also come in different __(10)__ , so some are weaker than others.

_____ **9.** A. sack   B. box   C. variety   D. cap

_____ **10.** A. zoos   B. strengths   C. rugs   D. letters

Part of Australia is a huge __(11)__ . People there live hundreds of miles apart. When someone got sick in the past, doctors were too far away to help. Then a group called the Flying Doctors got together. They wanted to __(12)__ sick people. Now doctors use radios for talking to people in need. The doctors use planes to take people to the hospital.

_____ **11.** A. water   B. pan   C. desert   D. street

_____ **12.** A. assist   B. meet   C. forget   D. splash

Many people think we'll live in space one day. Cities will be built inside big glass bubbles. We'll ride in __(13)__ as easily as we now ride in airplanes. Space life sounds very __(14)__ !

_____ **13.** A. horses   B. spaceships   C. land   D. boats

_____ **14.** A. merry   B. quiet   C. exciting   D. poor

A bog starts as a lake, pond, or slow-moving stream. The water gets trapped and can't __(15)__ . This leads to a __(16)__ of moss. Other plants start to die. The mosses and dead plants are a floating mat that becomes a bog.

_____ **15.** A. drain   B. fall   C. care   D. pay

_____ **16.** A. color   B. growth   C. pot   D. fence

Look in a mirror. That's glass on the front with silver on the __(1)__ side. The silver helps you see your __(2)__ . Glasses that darken in the sun have silver in them. Silver is in the wires of a TV. It may even be in your watch. You can see that silver has many uses.

_____ 1. **A.** even   **B.** reverse   **C.** dirty   **D.** odd

_____ 2. **A.** back   **B.** pine   **C.** neighbors   **D.** reflection

Each year many new toys are shown at the world's biggest toy fair. The fair is in Germany. It takes three days to see everything. There are games, dolls, and __(3)__ animals. Some toys are made in __(4)__ . Others are made by hand.

_____ 3. **A.** weak   **B.** gold   **C.** stuffed   **D.** low

_____ 4. **A.** factories   **B.** boxes   **C.** washers   **D.** tents

Forests don't grow only on land. They grow in the ocean, too. A large sea forest can cover many miles. __(5)__ of trees, the forests there are made of sea plants. The plants __(6)__ food and a home to many kinds of sea animals.

_____ 5. **A.** Thanks   **B.** Because   **C.** Instead   **D.** Knowing

_____ 6. **A.** find   **B.** provide   **C.** send   **D.** buy

Jerry Hammond had __(7)__ from a store and was sent to jail. When he got out, he looked at his life. His friends were in and out of jail. So he found some __(8)__ and moved in with them. He left his past behind. Now Jerry has a good job.

_____ 7. **A.** stolen   **B.** bought   **C.** seen   **D.** saved

_____ 8. **A.** pigs   **B.** stems   **C.** cars   **D.** relatives

What do you do when you spill salt? Do you throw some over your left side? Once people believed that a bad __(9)__ always stared over their left side. People were afraid that spilling salt would bring bad luck. So they threw the salt over their left side. And that is how this __(10)__ began.

_____ **9.** **A.** ten   **B.** card   **C.** spirit   **D.** soap

_____ **10.** **A.** fence   **B.** custom   **C.** drink   **D.** sand

---

In the 1920s cars were used more and more. They were also starting to go fast. And that meant __(11)__ ! Garrett Morgan made a machine that told drivers when to stop and go. It had __(12)__ red, green, and yellow lights.

_____ **11.** **A.** accidents   **B.** nests   **C.** sets   **D.** pins

_____ **12.** **A.** popping   **B.** flashing   **C.** eating   **D.** singing

---

A fawn lies hidden on the ground in the forest. Its spotted coat helps it stay hidden in the __(13)__ leaves. The fawn will stay very __(14)__ and quiet so it can't be heard by other animals.

_____ **13.** **A.** fallen   **B.** burning   **C.** last   **D.** thin

_____ **14.** **A.** lean   **B.** calm   **C.** sick   **D.** loud

---

Moths are insects with wings. There are many kinds of moths. They live just about everywhere. Moths are a lot like butterflies. It is often __(15)__ to tell them apart. Like butterflies, moths were once __(16)__ .

_____ **15.** **A.** usual   **B.** picky   **C.** difficult   **D.** tired

_____ **16.** **A.** rats   **B.** hens   **C.** pets   **D.** caterpillars

You might think of beavers as the (1) of the animal world. Beavers have strong front teeth. They cut down many trees. Beavers use the branches to build (2) for homes in the water. They use the bark for food.

_____ 1. **A.** keepers   **B.** lumberjacks   **C.** pilots   **D.** knights

_____ 2. **A.** lodges   **B.** pillows   **C.** motors   **D.** porches

---

The elf owl is most often found in dry areas of the country. It sits still in its nest during the day. Then the owl flies out to feed at (3) . It uses its (4) senses to find food.

_____ 3. **A.** market   **B.** sundown   **C.** breakfast   **D.** feather

_____ 4. **A.** flat   **B.** outside   **C.** fat   **D.** keen

---

BOLD is a group that helps blind people learn to ski. The helpers tell how the ski trail looks. They follow the skiers. They say when to turn. They teach other skiing (5) . The blind people ski on the same trails as (6) else.

_____ 5. **A.** skills   **B.** fiddles   **C.** hairs   **D.** stairs

_____ 6. **A.** all   **B.** somebody   **C.** everyone   **D.** someone

---

The king or queen of England owns the crown jewels. These (7) include crowns, rings, bracelets, (8) , and swords. They are kept safe in the Tower of London.

_____ 7. **A.** treasures   **B.** monkeys   **C.** carts   **D.** trails

_____ 8. **A.** tribes   **B.** doors   **C.** thoughts   **D.** necklaces

A *kibbutz* is a kind of large farm. Quite a few people in Israel live on them. During the day the children go to school. Their __(9)__ work on the kibbutz. Families __(10)__ the evenings together. Then the adults sleep in one house, and the children sleep in another.

_____ **9.** **A.** cameras   **B.** parents   **C.** donkeys   **D.** elves

_____ **10.** **A.** march   **B.** frown   **C.** float   **D.** share

---

Some countries have high-speed trains. These trains can __(11)__ high speeds for a long time. They can run at this __(12)__ because the track is very smooth and straight.

_____ **11.** **A.** leak   **B.** maintain   **C.** dive   **D.** wait

_____ **12.** **A.** shelf   **B.** pitch   **C.** arrow   **D.** pace

---

The Yellow Sea is off the east __(13)__ of China. The land around the sea has a yellow __(14)__ . Rivers and rainwater wash this soil to the sea. That's why the water looks yellow.

_____ **13.** **A.** rib   **B.** elevator   **C.** bath   **D.** coast

_____ **14.** **A.** flour   **B.** tint   **C.** evening   **D.** leaf

---

The royal antelope lives in western Africa. It is just ten inches tall. That makes it the smallest antelope in the world. This antelope is __(15)__ and hides most of the time. But it will run out in the open to get away from its __(16)__ !

_____ **15.** **A.** blue   **B.** lovely   **C.** shy   **D.** soft

_____ **16.** **A.** enemies   **B.** toast   **C.** chatter   **D.** neck

Three whales were found in the sea near Alaska. They were (1) in a hole in the ice. They couldn't (2) there for long. People couldn't get the whales to the open water. Then a ship that cuts through ice came. It cut a path through the ice. The whales used the path to return to the open sea.

_____ **1. A.** digging **B.** chased **C.** worn **D.** stranded

_____ **2. A.** march **B.** gaze **C.** survive **D.** reach

Tamarins are small monkeys. They live in Central and South American rain forests. There are 14 kinds of tamarins. Some kinds are (3) to live because people have (4) so much of the area where they live.

_____ **3. A.** born **B.** struggling **C.** begging **D.** planning

_____ **4. A.** destroyed **B.** printed **C.** weighed **D.** done

The hornbill is a bird. It looks (5) with its large, rounded bill. It lives in (6) in the forests of Africa and Asia. It eats mostly berries, fruits, and insects.

_____ **5. A.** clever **B.** wide **C.** stiff **D.** awkward

_____ **6. A.** treetops **B.** planes **C.** lakes **D.** cities

The sea peach is an animal that lives in the (7) of the sea. It has a round body with two holes. One hole takes in water and food. The other hole (8) water out.

_____ **7. A.** depths **B.** cracks **C.** dishes **D.** snow

_____ **8. A.** slaps **B.** gathers **C.** squirts **D.** strikes

Lynn Cox is a long-distance swimmer who has set many __(9)__ . She swam the English Channel. Then Lynn wanted to swim across the Bering Strait from Alaska to a Russian island. The Russians __(10)__ her swim. They greeted Lynn as she swam up to the island.

_____ **9. A.** bands   **B.** tables   **C.** fires   **D.** records

_____ **10. A.** began   **B.** approved   **C.** ate   **D.** did

---

Borneo is an island. Many villages there have only one house. It is called a longhouse. The people in the village live in the longhouse. They all have __(11)__ to do around the house. One person is __(12)__ head of the house.

_____ **11. A.** chores   **B.** bedrooms   **C.** mistakes   **D.** halls

_____ **12. A.** caught   **B.** marked   **C.** changed   **D.** elected

---

A lichen is really two plants. These plants become __(13)__ and work together. One plant makes the food for the pair. The other plant __(14)__ the water they need. Lichens grow in soil and on rocks and tree bark.

_____ **13. A.** rabbits   **B.** partners   **C.** uncles   **D.** fathers

_____ **14. A.** floats   **B.** imagines   **C.** absorbs   **D.** packs

---

Spices are made from parts of plants. They are used to __(15)__ food. Some spices improve the flavor of food. Others are used for the __(16)__ smell they give food.

_____ **15. A.** prove   **B.** roast   **C.** season   **D.** serve

_____ **16. A.** pleasant   **B.** brown   **C.** best   **D.** short

Skip It is a rope-jumping team. Nearly two hundred students belong to this group. Sometimes they do cartwheels and handstands while they jump. Sometimes they jump in pairs and **fling** each other up in the air. They even jump with two ropes at the same time. Their tricks are truly amazing.

_____ **1.** In this paragraph, the word **fling** means

    A. throw   **C.** trick

    B. wander   **D.** freeze

In Washington, D.C., there is a **memorial**. People call it the Wall. It helps us remember the men and women who died in the Vietnam War. Fifty-eight thousand Americans died in that war. All of their names are listed on the Wall.

_____ **2.** In this paragraph, the word **memorial** means

    A. building   **C.** reminder

    B. home   **D.** fortune

We have many different ways of measuring the weather. We can tell how hot or cold it is. We can see in which direction and at what **rate** the wind is blowing. We can tell how many inches of rain have fallen.

_____ **3.** In this paragraph, the word **rate** means

    A. base   **C.** chance

    B. sound   **D.** speed

Frances Allen made a bathtub for travelers. It was **portable**. Water went in and out through hoses. The plastic tub zipped up to keep the water and the person inside.

_____ **4.** In this paragraph, the word **portable** means

    A. sudden   **C.** movable

    B. sleepy   **D.** careless

Most people love to smell rose flowers. But did you know that some kinds of rose plants **produce** fruit? The fruit is called the hip. The rose plant makes hips after the flowers fall off. People use rose hips to make jelly and tea.

_____ **5.** In this paragraph, the word **produce** means

    A. call   **C.** round

    B. make   **D.** chop

In March 1986 six Americans started on a long, cold trip. They wanted to reach the North Pole. They took supplies on dog sleds. For eight weeks they traveled across ice in freezing weather. They had great courage and **endurance**. At last they made it! They were on top of the world.

_____ **6.** In this paragraph, the word **endurance** means

    A. many hours   **C.** lasting strength

    B. short steps   **D.** long rivers

On the island of Bermuda, people have a special day. They call it Kite Day. Everyone goes out to the fields and beaches to fly kites. Kites fill the sky. They **mask** the sun like bright clouds. They swoop like colorful airplanes.

_____ **7.** In this paragraph, the word **mask** means

    A. flap   **C.** save

    B. cut   **D.** cover

The sea snake lives in warm ocean waters. It breathes with special nostrils and lungs. It takes **oxygen** right out of the water. The sea snake can stay underwater for many hours.

_____ **8.** In this paragraph, the word **oxygen** means

    A. soil   **C.** exercise

    B. air   **D.** grain

One fish hunts for smaller fish by pretending to be something else. It **imitates** sea plants. It stands on its head and stays very still. Small fish swim among the sea plants. They don't see the fish until it is too late!

_____ **1.** In this paragraph, the word **imitates** means

    A. copies   **C.** understands

    B. stops   **D.** crosses

In the Middle Ages, life was very hard. So once a year people had a Fool's Party. They had the party to forget their **gloomy** lives. People did wild dances in the streets. They tried to forget their hunger.

_____ **2.** In this paragraph, the word **gloomy** means

    A. very easy   **C.** very sad

    B. very rich   **D.** very lazy

A man calls his dog Rock Hound because the dog has a real **ability** to find rocks! The man throws a rock onto a hill. The rock lands next to many other rocks. Rock Hound finds the right rock and brings it to the man.

_____ **3.** In this paragraph, the word **ability** means

    A. luck   **C.** skill

    B. course   **D.** sale

Most mouth organs are small enough to carry in your pocket. But the biggest one is 23 inches long! It has almost four hundred notes. You could play a pretty **melody** on that one. In fact, two people could play a song at the same time!

_____ **4.** In this paragraph, the word **melody** means

    A. tune   **C.** party

    B. game   **D.** hello

The ends of our fingers are covered with special lines. The lines are fingerprints. Fingerprints are like rubber **soles** on shoes. The rubber bumps on shoes keep us from falling down. The lines on our fingers help us hold things.

_____ **5.** In this paragraph, the word **soles** means

    A. checks   **C.** bottoms

    B. repairs   **D.** pockets

At first only men could dance on stage. One night a man could not dance. Marie Camargo got on stage and did the man's dance. The people who were watching were **thrilled**. When Camargo finished, they clapped and threw flowers on the stage. Now many stage dancers are women.

_____ **6.** In this paragraph, the word **thrilled** means

    A. delighted   **C.** awakened

    B. upset   **D.** broken

Lodestone is a natural magnet. Long ago, sailors used a piece of lodestone to tell which direction they were going. They tied the stone to a string. They **suspended** the stone in the air. It always pointed to the north.

_____ **7.** In this paragraph, the word **suspended** means

    A. crept   **C.** judged

    B. hung   **D.** grew

The toucan is a brightly colored bird. It makes its home in the Amazon forests. During the day it flies around looking for food. At night it **roosts** in a tree.

_____ **8.** In this paragraph, the word **roosts** means

    A. attacks   **C.** trusts

    B. wastes   **D.** rests

Larry Nyce builds tiny railroads. He makes the trains himself instead of **purchasing** them from a store. He lays the tracks on tiny wooden railroad ties. He makes tiny trees from sticks and little mountains from rocks.

_____ 1. In this paragraph, the word **purchasing** means
- A. selling
- B. riding
- C. buying
- D. carrying

One kind of lizard changes colors to match the thing it is standing on. These lizards can be green like leaves. They can be brown like tree bark. But if you put one on an apple, the lizard won't turn **scarlet**. It can match only the colors in its outdoor home.

_____ 2. In this paragraph, the word **scarlet** means
- A. shiny
- B. spotted
- C. red
- D. juicy

The Inca people lived five hundred years ago. Today some people remember the old Inca ways by dressing in Inca **costumes**. They wear hats with feathers on top and gold chains hanging down.

_____ 3. In this paragraph, the word **costumes** means
- A. clothes
- B. parades
- C. kings
- D. faces

The polar bear is a large bear with white fur. The polar bear's color helps it. The white fur blends with the white snow. The bear can **sneak** up on a seal without being seen.

_____ 4. In this paragraph, the word **sneak** means
- A. spill
- B. creep
- C. arrange
- D. hang

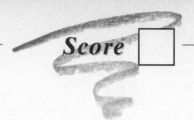
Look at the back of a dollar bill. You will find the words *In God We Trust*. This **motto** was first used on a coin. But it wasn't printed on paper money until 1957. Now it is printed on all United States paper money.

_____ **5.** In this paragraph, the word **motto** means

    A. puzzle   **C.** saying

    B. song   **D.** money

Fireflies aren't flies at all. They are beetles. These bugs can light up their bodies. The light **flickers** off and on. The flashing light signals other fireflies.

_____ **6.** In this paragraph, the word **flickers** means

    A. swims   **C.** shadows

    B. laughs   **D.** shines

The Ringling brothers started a very small circus. At first they did everything themselves. They made tents. They set up the circus acts. This **tough** life helped them become very famous. Now their "Greatest Show on Earth" goes all over the country.

_____ **7.** In this paragraph, the word **tough** means

    A. slow   **C.** old

    B. hard   **D.** hungry

The stingray uses its long tail to protect itself. On its tail is a sharp, poison hook. The hook can **pierce** an attacker's skin.

_____ **8.** In this paragraph, the word **pierce** means

    A. change into   **C.** go through

    B. look around   **D.** stay beside

Running is fun. Some people like to run against each other. But most people **prefer** to run against themselves. They may try to run more and more miles each day, or they may try to run for longer and longer times.

_____ **1.** In this paragraph, the word **prefer** means
  A. help   **C.** measure
  B. shop   **D.** like

Many animals live in shell houses, but they get their shells in different ways. A turtle's shell is really part of its skeleton. It wears its bones on the outside. A **clam** has no bones. It makes its shell from salt in the ocean.

_____ **2.** In this paragraph, the word **clam** means
  A. shark   **C.** small land animal
  B. fish   **D.** kind of sea animal

Babe Ruth was the home-run king for a long time. He hit a record 714 home runs. Ruth played his last game in 1935. Then he **retired**. It took almost forty years for someone to break his record.

_____ **3.** In this paragraph, the word **retired** means
  A. quit work   **C.** went to sleep
  B. played songs   **D.** forgot something

There are giant ships more than seven hundred feet long. These ships were built to carry tons of wheat from place to place. They have a road folded up in back. When they get to shore, the road unfolds. The **cargo** is moved on and off.

_____ **4.** In this paragraph, the word **cargo** means
  A. truck   **C.** load
  B. garbage   **D.** flower

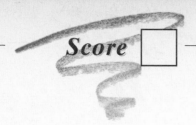
Your feet work hard. Each of your feet takes about ten thousand steps every day. Also, when you walk, you seem heavier than when you are standing still. With each step, your feet must **support** three times as many pounds! Why? Because walking is like falling. You keep your balance by falling onto the other foot.

_____ **5.** In this paragraph, the word **support** means

    A. hold up   **C.** run away

    B. sit still   **D.** stretch out

Long ago, people used natural things to make themselves clean and beautiful. They put eggs on their hair to make it shine. They washed in lemon juice to clean their skin. They **combined** honey and oats to make a special face soap.

_____ **6.** In this paragraph, the word **combined** means

    A. drove   **C.** tasted

    B. mixed   **D.** combed

Cattails are plants that grow in marshes. They are leafy with soft, flowering tops. Cattails make a **dense** cover. Many animals and birds hide in them.

_____ **7.** In this paragraph, the word **dense** means

    A. thick   **C.** woolen

    B. sweet   **D.** bent

The golden eagle lives on high peaks. It looks very **graceful** as it flies high in the sky. It catches the wind and seems to float in the air.

_____ **8.** In this paragraph, the word **graceful** means

    A. heavy   **C.** beautiful

    B. crowded   **D.** awful

Your body makes its own medicine. When you are **alarmed**, your body makes something that helps you run from trouble. When you are hurt, your body makes something that makes you hurt less.

_____ **1.** In this paragraph, the word **alarmed** means
- **A.** happy
- **B.** tall
- **C.** scared
- **D.** cold

In coal mines there is a gas that can kill people. Miners know how to stay clear of this gas. They use a safety lamp. The lamp's light **glows** blue when the gas is around. The miners watch the color of the flame. It shows the miners when to get out.

_____ **2.** In this paragraph, the word **glows** means
- **A.** feels
- **B.** sails
- **C.** burns
- **D.** adds

The poison arrow frog is found in South America. It has **vivid** colors on its skin. The frog's colorful skin warns birds not to eat it.

_____ **3.** In this paragraph, the word **vivid** means
- **A.** bright
- **B.** dull
- **C.** rotten
- **D.** painful

Penguins are birds, but they cannot fly. They use their wings to swim. They can also dive hundreds of feet down in the water to **search** for food. They like to find fish in cold, deep waters.

_____ **4.** In this paragraph, the word **search** means
- **A.** break
- **B.** look
- **C.** dance
- **D.** pay

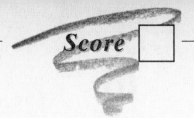
When you leave your house in the morning, it doesn't just stay the same. Sunlight falls on the rug. It warms the **fibers**, making them wave slowly. This waving warms the air and moves it around.

_____ **5.** In this paragraph, the word **fibers** means
- **A.** threads
- **B.** desks
- **C.** rooms
- **D.** walls

Both Americans and Japanese are told to fix their bad eating **habits**. But the people of these two countries have different problems to fix. Americans are told to cut down on fat. The Japanese have a problem with too much salt.

_____ **6.** In this paragraph, the word **habits** means
- **A.** forks
- **B.** ways
- **C.** friends
- **D.** caves

The kiwi is a bird that lives in New Zealand. The kiwi uses its good sense of smell to find food. Its **nostrils** are at the tip of its long, curved bill.

_____ **7.** In this paragraph, the word **nostrils** means
- **A.** eyes
- **B.** wings
- **C.** ears
- **D.** nose openings

The America's Cup is a boat race. It first started more than one hundred years ago. Boat builders in America had built a boat that they thought was much faster than the old kind. They sailed it across the sea and **challenged** the people there to a race. The new boat did win! The prize was a silver cup.

_____ **8.** In this paragraph, the word **challenged** means
- **A.** dared
- **B.** cooked
- **C.** hurried
- **D.** caged

The roadrunner is a bird. It is one of the fastest hunters in the desert. It can run up to twenty miles an hour. It moves so fast that it can kill a snake. The roadrunner's long legs also help it **flee** from its enemies.

_____ **1.** In this paragraph, the word **flee** means

    A. want   **C.** run

    B. know   **D.** set

A man had been in jail for most of his life. He decided to make a garden. He planted seeds and watered them. As the plants grew, he began to change. He changed from a **bitter** man to a very peaceful man. He said that working in the garden made him feel free.

_____ **2.** In this paragraph, the word **bitter** means

    A. jolly   **C.** steady

    B. angry   **D.** healthy

The skunk has a special way to protect itself. It sprays its enemies with a liquid from under its tail. This liquid has a **foul** smell. So the skunk is left alone.

_____ **3.** In this paragraph, the word **foul** means

    A. great   **C.** cloudy

    B. dandy   **D.** terrible

The leek is a plant like the onion. The people of Wales **respect** the leek. Long ago it helped them fight a war. They could not tell who was on their side. So the people from Wales put leeks in their caps.

_____ **4.** In this paragraph, the word **respect** means

    A. like   **C.** build

    B. melt   **D.** turn

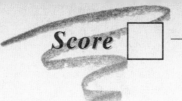
The most important part of a running shoe is the part under your foot. This bottom part must be thick and soft. That is so it will **cushion** your foot as you run. A good shoe can keep you running well for a long time.

_____ **5.** In this paragraph, the word **cushion** means
- **A.** bring
- **C.** protect
- **B.** tie
- **D.** enter

Sherlock Holmes is a great detective. But he lives only in books. The **tales** about him have been written in 57 languages.

_____ **6.** In this paragraph, the word **tales** means
- **A.** places
- **C.** stories
- **B.** names
- **D.** pens

Birds **perch** on a tree even while they sleep. Their toes grab the branch so they don't fall. Three toes point forward. One toe points backward. The toes lock tightly onto the branch.

_____ **7.** In this paragraph, the word **perch** means
- **A.** fly
- **C.** vanish
- **B.** sit
- **D.** promise

Doctors studied thousands of people. Some of the people spent most of their time alone. Many of these people had weak hearts. They were more likely to have a heart attack. Other people spent much time with their families and friends. Most of these **social** people had strong hearts.

_____ **8.** In this paragraph, the word **social** means
- **A.** lonely
- **C.** strange
- **B.** friendly
- **D.** sick

Car builders might make a new kind of car. The car will have a kind of **vision**. It will warn you if something is in your way. The car will be able to see a small child. It will be able to see a wall that is too close when you are parking.

_____ **1.** In this paragraph, the word **vision** means
- **A.** smell
- **B.** light
- **C.** sight
- **D.** window

Our eyes make different kinds of tears. One kind of tears keeps our eyes clean when we blink. Other tears fill our eyes when we cut onions. These tears **bathe** the onion juice from our eyes. Our eyes also make tears when we feel sad.

_____ **2.** In this paragraph, the word **bathe** means
- **A.** wash
- **B.** dry
- **C.** kiss
- **D.** lift

The armadillo can swim across a river. It **gulps** air into its stomach to make it float. Then it just paddles toward the other side!

_____ **3.** In this paragraph, the word **gulps** means
- **A.** heats
- **B.** plows
- **C.** shakes
- **D.** swallows

Sugar **arrived** in Europe hundreds of years ago. Traders brought it from the East. At first people used sugar as medicine. It was many years before people used sugar to make candy.

_____ **4.** In this paragraph, the word **arrived** means
- **A.** read
- **B.** came
- **C.** nodded
- **D.** tested

George Black had been making bricks by hand for a long time. He had started when he was 10 years old. He was the last person in the United States who could make bricks by hand. When he was 91, he went to South America and taught the people there his **craft**.

_____ **5.** In this paragraph, the word **craft** means

A. fit   **C.** skill

B. rock   **D.** yard

A man wanted a game that his whole family could play. He wanted a game that was **active** but not rough. He came up with a new game called hocker. He used parts of hockey and soccer. Hocker is played with a soft ball. There is much passing and running, but no hitting or blocking.

_____ **6.** In this paragraph, the word **active** means

A. lively   **C.** hollow

B. wise   **D.** rubber

The coot is a bird that lives near water. This bird flies with a great deal of **effort**. But it can swim and dive easily.

_____ **7.** In this paragraph, the word **effort** means

A. fun   **C.** hard work

B. bill   **D.** darkness

Skylab was a space station. It was in space for about six years. Other spacecraft **docked** with *Skylab*. Then people could enter *Skylab* from the spacecraft.

_____ **8.** In this paragraph, the word **docked** means

A. crashed   **C.** warned

B. folded   **D.** joined

Few plants grow on mountaintops. But some plants do find a way to live in these cold places. A few **sturdy** trees might plant their roots between two rocks. They find a way to hang on in the strong winds and heavy snows.

_____ **1.** In this paragraph, the word **sturdy** means

    A. mean   **C.** strong

    B. dead   **D.** wrong

Basketball used to be a slow game. Players always used two hands to **heave** the ball into the basket. They always kept their feet on the ground when they made a shot.

_____ **2.** In this paragraph, the word **heave** means

    A. throw   **C.** think

    B. bake   **D.** grow

A man hit his head when he was getting into the car. Then he hit it again on the kitchen cupboard. He hit his head three more times in one week. He seemed fine after this **series** of accidents. Then one night he couldn't remember anything. He did not even know where he lived.

_____ **3.** In this paragraph, the word **series** means

    A. baseball   **C.** several in a row

    B. mad   **D.** too many to count

Building the railroads was hard work. The workers would sing to make their **labor** seem easier.

_____ **4.** In this paragraph, the word **labor** means

    A. steps   **C.** train

    B. work   **D.** tune

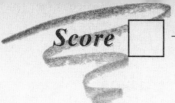

Ferns are plants without flowers. Most ferns live in **mild** climates, but some ferns can grow in cold places.

_____ **5.** In this paragraph, the word **mild** means
- **A.** warm
- **B.** cheerful
- **C.** noisy
- **D.** sour

A man wanted to be the first to see a desert that had never been explored. He bought two camels and set out. The trip took 19 days. He got lost and ran out of water. He was **exhausted** from walking in the heat. He lost 60 pounds. But finally he made it!

_____ **6.** In this paragraph, the word **exhausted** means
- **A.** very shy
- **B.** very tired
- **C.** very afraid
- **D.** very ready

Some jungle animals travel by air. They may look as if they are flying, but they're not. They're gliding. They leap from a high branch and **descend** to a lower branch.

_____ **7.** In this paragraph, the word **descend** means
- **A.** go down
- **B.** fly by
- **C.** jump up
- **D.** cross over

The tiger cat lives in Australia. It runs fast and also climbs trees well. The tiger cat looks for small animals at night. This cat hunts **restlessly** until it catches its dinner.

_____ **8.** In this paragraph, the word **restlessly** means
- **A.** in cities
- **B.** under water
- **C.** while sleeping
- **D.** without stopping

Catnip is a plant. It belongs to the mint family. It grows wild along many roads. Cats love to roll and play in catnip. They also like to eat it. They like the **taste** of the plant.

_____ **1.** In this paragraph, the word **taste** means

   A. fear   **C.** flavor

   B. dash   **D.** example

In 1888 there was a terrible **blizzard** in New York City. It lasted for three days. There were strong winds. Blowing snow was all that could be seen. Many people died in this storm.

_____ **2.** In this paragraph, the word **blizzard** means

   A. house   **C.** guard

   B. rain   **D.** snowstorm

People have **measured** time in many ways. At first, people used the sun, moon, and stars to tell time. Now we use clocks to keep track of time.

_____ **3.** In this paragraph, the word **measured** means

   A. closed   **C.** found the length of

   B. opened   **D.** put in a bottle

The glass snake is not a snake at all. It is a lizard without legs. Its tail is twice the length of its body. The glass snake can **shed** its tail if it is attacked. A new tail will grow in its place.

_____ **4.** In this paragraph, the word **shed** means

   A. fool   **C.** puff up

   B. lose   **D.** take in

Lapland is a region in the far north of Europe and Russia. The people, called Lapps, keep herds of reindeer. They use the reindeer to meet almost all of their needs. The Lapps live in tents. They cover the tent frames with reindeer **hides**.

_____ **5.** In this paragraph, the word **hides** means

    A. food   **C.** harnesses

    B. skins   **D.** mountains

The killdeer is a type of bird. It has a special way to protect its chick. If the killdeer sees an enemy, it will **pretend** it has a broken wing. It leads the enemy far away. Then the bird flies back to the chick.

_____ **6.** In this paragraph, the word **pretend** means

    A. act as if   **C.** find out that

    B. jump until   **D.** look to see whether

One type of insect is helpful to farmers. It eats worms and other insects that destroy plants. This helpful insect is **seldom** seen since it lives underground.

_____ **7.** In this paragraph, the word **seldom** means

    A. often   **C.** yesterday

    B. exactly   **D.** hardly ever

Rita Moreno can sing, dance, and act. She has also worked hard. Rita has won **awards** for her work in movies, TV, and theater.

_____ **8.** In this paragraph, the word **awards** means

    A. records   **C.** honors

    B. circles   **D.** directions

Trees are important. Their roots help hold soil in place and keep it from being washed away by rains. Tree roots also help hold **moisture** in the ground and keep it from drying out.

_____ **1.** In this paragraph, the word **moisture** means

    A. cloth   **C.** dampness

    B. morning   **D.** safety

A blimp is a small airship. It doesn't have a metal frame to give it shape. But a blimp does have a strong bag that is filled with gas. The gas makes the blimp float. When the gas is taken out, the blimp **collapses**.

_____ **2.** In this paragraph, the word **collapses** means

    A. falls down   **C.** flies off

    B. works out   **D.** takes over

There is a huge copper mine in Utah. The mine is an open pit. It is about half a mile deep and more than two miles wide at the top. This mine has **yielded** more copper than any other mine.

_____ **3.** In this paragraph, the word **yielded** means

    A. bowed   **C.** stretched

    B. supplied   **D.** divided

Baby geese are called goslings. The mother goose does not have to teach them how to behave like geese. The goslings can swim and dive without **instruction**.

_____ **4.** In this paragraph, the word **instruction** means

    A. frogs   **C.** crowns

    B. books   **D.** lessons

Poon Lim was alone in the Atlantic Ocean. It was World War II. The British ship he was on had just been sunk. He got on the ship's **raft**. He drifted for more than four months. He lived on fish and rain water. Finally he was picked up by a passing ship.

_____ **5.** In this paragraph, the word **raft** means
- **A.** balloon
- **C.** small boat
- **B.** flag
- **D.** long pole

Mammoths lived during the Ice Age. They looked like elephants with curved tusks, but their bodies were covered with long hair. This hair protected the mammoths from the **severe** cold.

_____ **6.** In this paragraph, the word **severe** means
- **A.** very gentle
- **C.** most famous
- **B.** quite warm
- **D.** very bad

The pangolin lives in Asia and Africa. Its body is covered with sharp-edged scales that protect it. If this shy creature becomes frightened, it **merely** rolls itself into a tight ball.

_____ **7.** In this paragraph, the word **merely** means
- **A.** nightly
- **C.** coldly
- **B.** simply
- **D.** darkly

Truffles are tasty plants. They are hard to find because they grow underground. People train dogs and pigs to hunt for truffles. Dogs and pigs have a good sense of smell. They find these plants by their **odor**.

_____ **8.** In this paragraph, the word **odor** means
- **A.** color
- **C.** scent
- **B.** feel
- **D.** taste

Piranhas are fish. They live in South American rivers. These fish tend to swim in large groups. They will tear the flesh off an animal or person that gets in the water. In just minutes all that is left is the **skeleton**.

_____ **1.** In this paragraph, the word **skeleton** means
- **A.** key
- **B.** pie
- **C.** butter
- **D.** bones

A cartoon is a **humorous** way to tell a story or make a point. A cartoon can be one drawing or a set of drawings. A cartoon may have words with the picture. But words aren't always needed.

_____ **2.** In this paragraph, the word **humorous** means
- **A.** cozy
- **B.** funny
- **C.** dangerous
- **D.** thirsty

Pluto is the planet farthest from the sun. Not much is known about this **distant** planet. It is quite cold there since it is so far from the sun. Scientists don't think that there is any life on Pluto.

_____ **3.** In this paragraph, the word **distant** means
- **A.** faraway
- **B.** nearby
- **C.** lucky
- **D.** pleasant

Long ago, **vessels** crossed the water from northern Europe to other countries. They carried Viking warriors. At first the Vikings fought with people. Then the Vikings decided to trade. They set up many new trade centers.

_____ **4.** In this paragraph, the word **vessels** means
- **A.** whales
- **B.** bottles
- **C.** ships
- **D.** horses

The bush baby lives in African forests. It sleeps during the day. At night it wakens from its **slumber**. The bush baby has large eyes. It can see in the dark. It leaps among tree branches to find food.

_____ **5.** In this paragraph, the word **slumber** means
- **A.** sleep
- **B.** lunch
- **C.** log
- **D.** address

Mary Walker was a doctor. During the Civil War, she treated **injured** soldiers. Mary was named Assistant Surgeon in the United States Army. She was the first woman to hold this job.

_____ **6.** In this paragraph, the word **injured** means
- **A.** fair
- **B.** six
- **C.** early
- **D.** hurt

An android is a type of **robot**. It looks like a person, but its brain is a computer. The android is made to do jobs. These jobs are not safe for people to do.

_____ **7.** In this paragraph, the word **robot** means
- **A.** apartment
- **B.** machine
- **C.** berry
- **D.** mirror

Benin was once a strong **kingdom** in Africa. It held much power from the 1400s through the 1600s. The people of Benin made metal statues to honor their rulers. These works of art are now famous all over the world.

_____ **8.** In this paragraph, the word **kingdom** means
- **A.** cabin
- **B.** costume
- **C.** country
- **D.** painting

Wild flowers grow in many **environments**. Some are found in woods or fields. Others grow on mountains or in streams and ponds. Wild flowers can grow in the desert, too.

_____ **1.** In this paragraph, the word **environments** means

    A. blossoms   **C.** oceans

    B. settings   **D.** insects

Some Americans want to help others. They join the Peace Corps. These workers go to other nations. They try to **educate** the people to help themselves.

_____ **2.** In this paragraph, the word **educate** means

    A. present   **C.** hurry

    B. bounce   **D.** teach

At one time women could not vote or own land. Susan B. Anthony knew that women didn't have the same rights as men. She worked hard to **obtain** equal rights for women. But it was not until many years after her death that women finally won these rights.

_____ **3.** In this paragraph, the word **obtain** means

    A. follow   **C.** get

    B. notice   **D.** move

Sometimes a huge **mass** of ice breaks off from a glacier. It falls into the sea and floats. This block of ice is called an iceberg. Ships must be careful of icebergs.

_____ **4.** In this paragraph, the word **mass** means

    A. shade   **C.** block

    B. tooth   **D.** church

Jacques Cousteau is famous for his studies of the oceans. To help him in his studies, he has come up with many ways to stay underwater. He made a **vehicle** that can move underwater. It is called a diving saucer. People can ride in it under the sea for a long time.

_____ **5.** In this paragraph, the word **vehicle** means

    A. radio   **C.** case

    B. something used   **D.** something used
       for eating   for traveling

The fifth of May is a special day in Japan. It is known as Children's Day. There is a big **festival** on this day. All boys and girls are honored on Children's Day.

_____ **6.** In this paragraph, the word **festival** means

    A. party   **C.** egg

    B. bench   **D.** spider

The musk ox lives in the far north, in Alaska, Canada, and Greenland. The musk ox has a shaggy **appearance**. It is covered with long, brown hair. The hair keeps it warm in the cold and snow.

_____ **7.** In this paragraph, the word **appearance** means

    A. village   **C.** look

    B. model   **D.** ticket

The swordfish lives in warm seas. It has a long, flat upper jaw that looks like a sword. The swordfish has been known to **ram** holes in ships with its sword.

_____ **8.** In this paragraph, the word **ram** means

    A. feed   **C.** hear

    B. knock   **D.** write

The frogfish has an easy way to **capture** a small fish. The frogfish has a fishing pole that it waves above its mouth. The small fish swims to the pole. Then the frogfish eats the small fish.

_____ **1.** In this paragraph, the word **capture** means

    A. paste   **C.** forget

    B. catch   **D.** frighten

The fennec fox is the smallest fox, but it has the largest ears. This fox uses its large ears to listen for insects. It can hear an insect's **movements** in the sand. The fox eats the insects it finds.

_____ **2.** In this paragraph, the word **movements** means

    A. arms   **C.** motions

    B. parks   **D.** seasons

Maria Mitchell studied the skies for years. Maria found a new comet. She was **awarded** a gold medal.

_____ **3.** In this paragraph, the word **awarded** means

    A. forced   **C.** arrived

    B. given   **D.** poured

The largest insect in the world lives in Africa. It is called the Goliath beetle. Although it is so large, it is quite **harmless**. African children often use the beetle as a toy.

_____ **4.** In this paragraph, the word **harmless** means

    A. alike   **C.** yellow

    B. quick   **D.** safe

The Negev Desert covers half of Israel. The soil in this desert is **fertile**. People can grow crops there. They use water from a nearby sea. Special hoses spray water on the crops.

_____ **5.** In this paragraph, the word **fertile** means
- **A.** rich
- **B.** glad
- **C.** greedy
- **D.** sharp

The bluebonnet is one flower that really helps bees. A bluebonnet has a white spot on it. After a bee has visited this flower and taken nectar, the white spot turns red. The other bees don't waste time. They know they will be **disappointed** if they go to the blue flowers with red spots.

_____ **6.** In this paragraph, the word **disappointed** means
- **A.** pretty
- **B.** hot
- **C.** large
- **D.** sorry

The Aztecs lived long ago. They were a great tribe. They built a **glorious** city. Now this city is known as Mexico City.

_____ **7.** In this paragraph, the word **glorious** means
- **A.** foolish
- **B.** grand
- **C.** corner
- **D.** helpless

Plants can be grown without soil. They grow in special water. The water has everything that plants need to grow. This **style** of farming is called hydroponics. It can be used in space.

_____ **8.** In this paragraph, the word **style** means
- **A.** center
- **B.** garden
- **C.** rush
- **D.** type

Think and Apply

What's the Word?

Each of the sentences on this page is missing a word. Read the sentences. Choose a word from the box to go in each sentence. Write the word on the line.

mumble	prairie	collar	mystery
orchards	score	closet	scissors

1. You have to button your _____ to wear a tie.

2. Grace's mother said, "Please don't _____ . I can't understand you."

3. These _____ are so sharp that they will cut through metal.

4. Something that cannot be explained is a _____ .

5. The runner crossed the base to _____ a point.

6. I keep my clothes in the _____ .

7. The buffalo used to live on the _____ in great numbers.

8. Many fruit trees grow in _____ .

To check your answers, turn to page 62.

A Context Puzzle

Read each sentence. Think of a word that fits the context and the space. Write the word on the lines. Then match the numbered letters to the squares on the puzzle. When you finish the puzzle correctly, you will know a new fact.

1. A tool for chopping wood is
   an _____ .

   __ __
   1a 1b

2. If you get away or get free,
   you _____ .

   __ __ __ __ __ __
   2a 2b 2c 2d 2e 2f

3. A fish uses its _____ to swim.

   __ __ __
   3a 3b 3c

4. I _____ in a chair yesterday.

   __ __ __
   4a 4b 4c

5. "Come with _____ !" said Al and Deb.

   __ __
   5a 5b

6. Round pieces of ice that fall
   from the sky are called _____ .

   __ __ __ __
   6a 6b 6c 6d

7. Joe looked at the thing in front
   of him. "What is _____ ?" he asked.

   __ __
   7a 7b

8. A toddler is sometimes called
   a _____ .

   __ __ __
   8a 8b 8c

1a	5a	4a	4c	6c	3c		3b	5b		
7b	6a	2a		2c	4b	2e	7a	8c	2d	6d
	8b	3a		8a	2f	1b	6b	2b		

A Strange Adventure

Read the story. Find the ten words that do not make sense in the context of the story. Draw a line through those words. On the lines below the story, list ten words that would make more sense in the story context.

Jan got ready to leave on the camping trip. She filled her backpack and packed her tent. She tied her piano to the top of the van. She took some ducks to eat along the way.

She drove along the busy map on her way to Hi-Ho Camp. She sang her favorite newspapers. She thought about the mice who would be waiting for her at the camp. What a terrible time they would have swimming, fishing, and cooking over the camp hammer!

After a few years, Jan reached the little road that led to the camp. She drove under the tall green people. She knew this would be the most exciting nap she had ever had.

1. _____

2. _____

3. _____

4. _____

5. _____

6. _____

7. _____

8. _____

9. _____

10. _____

To check your answers, turn to page 62.

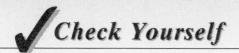

Unit *1* pp. 6-7	Unit *2* pp. 8-9	Unit *3* pp. 10-11	Unit *4* pp. 12-13	Unit *5* pp. 14-15	Unit *6* pp. 16-17	Unit *7* pp. 18-19	Unit *8* pp. 20-21
1. D	1. A	1. C	1. C	1. D	1. C	1. C	1. B
2. A	2. B	2. A	2. B	2. C	2. B	2. B	2. A
3. A	3. C	3. B	3. D	3. D	3. C	3. C	3. C
4. B	4. B	4. D	4. C	4. A	4. A	4. A	4. C
5. D	5. A	5. C	5. B	5. D	5. C	5. B	5. B
6. C	6. B	6. A	6. A	6. A	6. D	6. A	6. D
7. B	7. A	7. B	7. C	7. B	7. B	7. B	7. D
8. D	8. D	8. B	8. D	8. C	8. C	8. B	8. B
9. A	9. B	9. C	9. D	9. C	9. B	9. D	9. B
10. C	10. A	10. D	10. B	10. A	10. D	10. A	10. A
11. B	11. C	11. B	11. A	11. B	11. A	11. A	11. D
12. A	12. C	12. C	12. D	12. C	12. C	12. C	12. A
13. C	13. D	13. C	13. B	13. B	13. D	13. C	13. A
14. D	14. B	14. B	14. A	14. C	14. B	14. A	14. C
15. C	15. D	15. A	15. C	15. C	15. D	15. B	15. B
16. A	16. B	16. C	16. B	16. B	16. A	16. D	16. B

Unit 9 pp. 22-23	Unit 10 pp. 24-25	Unit 11 pp. 26-27	Unit 12 pp. 28-29	Unit 13 pp. 30-31	Unit 14 pp. 32-33	Unit 15 pp. 34-35	Unit 16 pp. 36-37
1. B	1. B	1. B	1. D	1. A	1. A	1. C	1. D
2. C	2. D	2. A	2. C				
3. B	3. C	3. B	3. B	2. C	2. C	2. C	2. D
4. A	4. A	4. D	4. A				
5. D	5. C	5. A	5. D	3. D	3. C	3. A	3. A
6. B	6. B	6. C	6. A				
7. D	7. A	7. A	7. A	4. C	4. A	4. B	4. C
8. C	8. D	8. D	8. C				
9. C	9. C	9. B	9. D	5. B	5. C	5. C	5. A
10. B	10. B	10. D	10. B				
11. C	11. A	11. B	11. A	6. C	6. A	6. D	6. B
12. A	12. B	12. D	12. D				
13. B	13. A	13. D	13. B	7. D	7. B	7. B	7. A
14. C	14. B	14. B	14. C				
15. A	15. C	15. C	15. C	8. B	8. D	8. C	8. C
16. B	16. D	16. A	16. A				

Unit 17 pp. 38-39	Unit 18 pp. 40-41	Unit 19 pp. 42-43	Unit 20 pp.44-45	Unit 21 pp. 46-47	Unit 22 pp. 48-49	Unit 23 pp. 50-51	Unit 24 pp. 52-53	Unit 25 pp. 54-55
1. C	1. C	1. C	1. C	1. C	1. C	1. D	1. B	1. B
2. C	2. B	2. A	2. A	2. D	2. A	2. B	2. D	2. C
3. A	3. D	3. D	3. C	3. C	3. B	3. A	3. C	3. B
4. B	4. A	4. B	4. B	4. B	4. D	4. C	4. C	4. D
5. A	5. C	5. C	5. A	5. B	5. C	5. A	5. D	5. A
6. B	6. C	6. A	6. B	6. A	6. D	6. D	6. A	6. D
7. D	7. B	7. C	7. A	7. D	7. B	7. B	7. C	7. B
8. A	8. B	8. D	8. D	8. C	8. C	8. C	8. B	8. D

Working with Context, Page 4

2. A

3. C

What's the Word? Page 56

1. collar

5. score

2. mumble

6. closet

3. scissors

7. prairie

4. mystery

8. orchards

A Context Puzzle, Page 57

1. ax

5. us

2. escape

6. hail

3. fin

7. it

4. sat

8. tot

Answer to puzzle: Austin is the capital of Texas.

A Strange Adventure, Page 58

The ten words that do not fit the context include the following: *piano*, *ducks*, *map*, *newspapers*, *mice*, *terrible*, *hammer*, *years*, *people*, and *nap*.

Some possible substitute words include the following:

1. tent

6. great

2. snacks

7. fire

3. road

8. hours

4. songs

9. trees

5. friends

10. vacation